My eight Book

by Jane Belk Moncure
illustrated by Linda Hohag
and Dan Spoden

THE CHILD'S WORLD

Library of Congress Cataloging in Publication Data

Moncure, Jane Belk.
  My eight book.

  (My number books / Jane Belk Moncure)
  Summary: Little Eight introduces the concept
of "eight" by interacting with eight of a number of
things, Some of which are grouped to further expose
the reader to subtracting and dividing.
  1. Eight (The number)—Juvenile literature.
[1. Eight (The number) 2. Number concept.
3. Counting]   I. Hohag, Linda, ill.   II. Title.
III Title: My 8 book.IV.   Series: Moncure, Jane
Belk. My number books.
QA141.3.M673 1986   513'.2 [E]   85-30962
ISBN 0-89565-319-6 -1995 Edition

© 1986 The Child's World, Inc.
All rights reserved. Printed in U.S.A.

Grolier Books is a Division of Grolier Enterprises, Inc.

My  Book

This is Little **eight**

Little  lives in the house of eight.

It has eight rooms. Count them.

Every day Little  goes for a walk. One day she walks to a farm. She sees a

mama hen.

Then she sees seven
little yellow babies . . .

pop out from under the mama's wings.
How many are in the whole family?

Little  opens a gate. She sees

two brown goats,

two black goats,

and four
white goats in a pen.

How many all together?

Little  eight opens the gate very wide.
How many goats run outside?

How many goats stay in the pen?

Just then the farm dog runs by. He chases . . .

two goats

back into the pen.

Little  counts the goats.

How many are missing?

Then two more goats run back
through the gate.

Does Little count eight goats?

Little **eight** hops to a grapevine. "I will pick a bunch with eight grapes," she says.

Which bunch does she pick?

Next Little  skips into the garden.

She picks two tomatoes,

two cucumbers,

two carrots,

 one head of lettuce,

and one radish 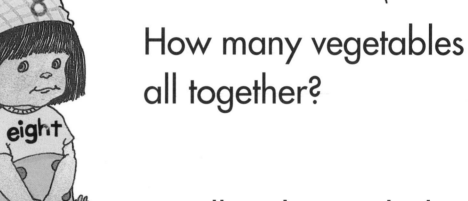 .

How many vegetables all together?

"I will make a salad," she says.

Little  makes a very big salad.
She invites her bunny friends
to a picnic.

How many bunnies come?

"Let's play hide-and-seek," says one bunny.

Little eight closes her eyes. She counts to eight very fast. Can you?

Away hop the bunnies.

Little **eight** finds five bunnies

behind some bushes. How many bunnies are still hiding?

Then Little  eight finds three bunnies in a field of daisies. Has Little eight found all the bunnies?

"What pretty daisies," says Little  .
"I will give each bunny a daisy."

Little eight picks a bunch of six daisies.

How many more does Little eight need?

The happy bunnies hop eight hops.
Can you?

Guess where the bunnies go?

The bunnies hop to the Easter Bunny's workshop.

Little

peeks in the window.

She sees bunches of colored eggs.

Little  sees bunches of chocolate bunnies and

bunches of marshmallow chicks.

She counts many bunches of things. Can you?

The bunnies give Little  eight a basket.

One bunny says "You may take eight things."

Little eight puts four colored eggs in her basket.

She puts

two chocolate bunnies
in her basket.

How many marshmallow chicks does Little
take to make eight things?

One, two, or three?

"Thank you and goodbye," says Little
to her bunny friends.

When she gets home,
she invites her best
friend to a tea party.

"I will share my Easter basket with you," says Little  . "Two eggs for you, two eggs for me. One chick for you, one chick for me."

How does she share the chocolate bunnies?

Let's add with Little eight.

$$\begin{array}{r} 7 \\ +1 \\ \hline 8 \end{array}$$

$$\begin{array}{r} 6 \\ +2 \\ \hline 8 \end{array}$$

$$\begin{array}{r} 5 \\ +3 \\ \hline 8 \end{array}$$

$$\begin{array}{r} 4 \\ +4 \\ \hline 8 \end{array}$$

Now you add eight things together in other ways.

Let's take away with Little eight.

$$\begin{array}{r} 8 \\ -1 \\ \hline 7 \end{array}$$

$$\begin{array}{r} 8 \\ -2 \\ \hline 6 \end{array}$$

$$\begin{array}{r} 8 \\ -3 \\ \hline 5 \end{array}$$

$$\begin{array}{r} 8 \\ -4 \\ \hline 4 \end{array}$$

Now you find other ways to take away from eight.

Extra Pages

Little  makes an 8 this way:

Then she makes the number word like this:

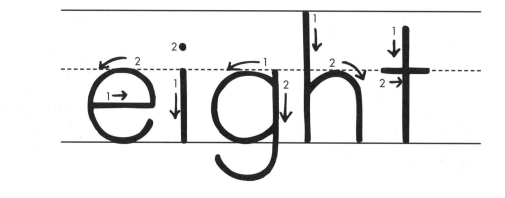

You can make them in the air with your finger.